INFLATION

Learn What It Is, What Assets Provide Maximum Protection and How You Can Profit From It.

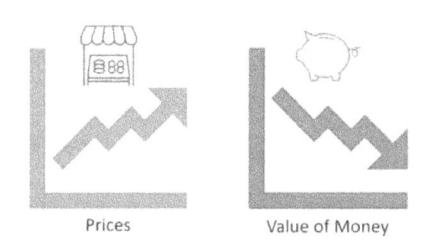

Alexander W. Young

Copyright 2022 – Alexander W. Young

All rights reserved. No part of this guide may be reproduced in any form without permission in writing from the publisher except in the case of brief quotations embodied in critical articles or reviews.

Published by:

Valleywide Publishing
8600 Tyler Blvd #1801
Mentor OH 44061

Legal & Disclaimer

The information contained in this book and its contents is not designed to replace or take the place of any form of medical or professional advice; and is not meant to replace the need for independent medical, financial, legal or other professional advice or services, as may be required. The content and information in this book has been provided for educational and entertainment purposes only.

The content and information contained in this book has been compiled from sources deemed reliable, and it is accurate to the best of the Author's knowledge, information and belief. However, the Author cannot guarantee its accuracy and validity and cannot be held liable for any errors and/or omissions. Further, changes are periodically made to this book as and when needed. Where appropriate and/or necessary, you must consult a professional (including but not limited to your doctor, attorney, financial advisor or such other professional advisor) before using any of the suggested remedies, techniques, or information in this book.

Upon using the contents and information contained in this

book, you agree to hold harmless the Author from and against any damages, costs, and expenses, including any legal fees potentially resulting from the application of any of the information provided by this book. This disclaimer applies to any loss, damages or injury caused by the use and application, whether directly or indirectly, of any advice or information presented, whether for breach of contract, tort, negligence, personal injury, criminal intent, or under any other cause of action.

You agree to accept all risks of using the information presented inside this book.

You agree that by continuing to read this book, where appropriate and/or necessary, you shall consult a professional (including but not limited to your doctor, attorney, or financial advisor or such other advisor as needed) before using any of the suggested remedies, techniques, or information in this book.

Table of Contents

Introduction

What causes inflation?

Demand-Pull Effect

Cost-Push Effect

Built-In Inflation

Chapter 1: Inflation and the money supply theory

History of the theory

The key formula

Quantity theory of money

Evidence for the theory

Some issues with the theory

Money supply and asset price inflation

Two separate money supplies? Two separate inflations?

Chapter 2: China Dominating The New World Order since 2016

Why is the Economy of China Growing so Fast?

- What are the Consequences for the US?
- What will Happen to the Dollar as the World's Reserve Currency?

The Most Valuable Financial Secret In The World
- Why Is The Gold Standard So Important?
- History and Effectiveness of the Modern Age Gold Standard
- Timeless Store of Value Provides Immunity to Financial Busts
- No Way to Protect Savings from Inflation Without Gold Standard
- Excessive Debt Burden Leads to Hyperinflation or Default
- The Debt Load Began To Explode
- Is the Gold Standard Still Practical Today?

Save Your Financial Assets From The Gathering Storm
- About the Authors Jeff Cox and Peter J. Tanous

What is the Premise of the Book?

The Euro Devaluation Will Continue

Retirement Payments Will Stop

What Has Caused the Problems?

What Does the Book Predict?

What Can You Do to Protect Yourself Personally?

Verdict of the Book

E-Inflation

Chapter 3: Price stability and the consolidation period

A new monetary system: Chicago or bust

The block chain world

Inflation would never disappear

Implications for pay and inequality

Implications for business

Chapter 4: The Strategies Employed in Forex Trading

Fundamental analysis

Interest rates

- Employment
- GDP
- Prices of commodities
- Weather conditions
- Technical analysis
  - Moving averages
  - Bollinger bands
  - Stochastic oscillator
  - Fibonacci retracements
  - Sentimental analysis
  - Forex hedging against inflation

Chapter 5: Will Bitcoin takes over the US Dollar?

Chapter 6: Lending Protocol for Crypto Loans

Chapter 7: Cryptocurrencies

- Bitcoin as an Asset Class and an Investment
- Litecoin and Ethereum

Historical Performance Against Inflation

Prospects as a Hedge Against Inflation

Chapter 8: Worst case scenario - Hyperinflation

What causes hyperinflation?

Options for Hyperinflation

Owning Farmland or a Home Garden

Converting Everything to Foreign Currency or Precious Metals

Postponing Payment of Debt

Getting into Long Term Financing

The Risk of Government Intervention

Conclusion

Sectors that Outperform during Inflationary Periods

The Importance of Diversification in a Portfolio

Introduction

"The more things change, the more they remain the same."

But does this apply to Inflation?

We haven't seen serious economic Inflation since the 1970's when interest rates went into the teens; Consumer and commodity prices soared beyond belief.

Why?

What's really going on, aren't we due for real Inflation?

Is it possible the Federal Reserve really has been holding it back with tremendous quantitative easing and money printing?

Or is it that we are actually in a Deflationary cycle and all the actions by the Fed to incur Inflation are simply holding us steady.

As a small investor, I definitely want Deflation, since that's where the Dollar increases in value and asset prices crash, thus allowing "main street" investors to finally buy assets at bargain prices (real estate, stocks, commodities, personal items, land, etc..)

Ever get the feeling like groceries keep getting more and more expensive, as well as other common things we purchase daily?

Does it feel like someone is secretly taxing you when you purchase common items? Why does everything keep getting more expensive? Who and what is causing this?

Food, housing prices, rents, technology, gas, utilities, clothing, investments, stocks, metals, commodities; all of these things are affected **by Economic Inflation**.

In this book we will explore how this happens, who benefits from it and how you can profit and protect yourself from..

INFLATION is often created by design and on purpose by banks and governments. It benefits the ultra rich and governments, yet decimates the middle income classes and small businesses.

History indeed repeats itself over and over. Assuredly, monetary Inflation will return. But will it be like in the past? Probably not.

In a way, Inflation is already here. It is only in certain assets, such as stocks and real estate. Our world is changing at a rapid pace every day. This means that you must be able to pivot your investment and financial strategies quickly and be able to adapt to changing economies as they occur.

Inflation can steal your money from you, it is a hidden tax from the governments designed to take your money right from your bank accounts and pockets, by increased asset prices and dwindling US dollar purchasing power.

Are there ways you can hedge against this?

YES, but you must implement these strategies as soon as possible and very strategically.

How do you make money from an Inflationary economic environment?

There are many techniques you can use from bonds, equities, certain real estate classes and even buying and selling consumer goods.

As you may have heard, the worst thing you can do is leave your money in a cash checking account doing nothing. Savings accounts get wiped out during Inflationary times. You have to get your money working for you.

The 80/20 Reality of Economic Inflation

What are the worst outcomes of Economic Inflation?

1. The value of the Dollar decreases drastically.
2. The purchasing power of Dollars falls worldwide.
3. Exports decrease, imports increase.
4. Hard Asset prices increase.
5. Stock equities increase in price.

6. Commodity prices increase.

7. Interest rates typically go up to stop Inflation, unless the government wants Inflation.

8. Taxes increase.

9. Rents increase.

10. Housing prices increase.

11. Gas and oil prices increase.

12. Food prices increase.

13. The middle class is destroyed.

14. There is only the Rich and the Poor.

What are the hidden benefits of Economic Inflation?

1. Debts get paid off faster.

2. Mortgages and debt decrease in balance faster.

3. Sellers of real estate achieve higher prices.

4. Stock sellers win in certain sectors.

5. High interest-bearing bank accounts may become available, if interest rates are increased by government.

6. Landlords get higher rents, but also higher expenses.

Inflation explained simply

Inflation is the rate at which a currency experiences a decrease in its purchasing power. It happens over a long period in most economies. However, there are examples of very high inflation rates over short periods, known as hyperinflation. Economists argue that inflation is almost always a result of an excessive increase in the money supply in an economy.

The general population feels inflation by the increase in the prices of goods they purchase. Things like groceries, fuel, and utilities get expensive over the length of time when an economy is experiencing inflation. Each unit of that economy's currency loses its value in terms of what people can exchange it for. When economies continue to suffer relatively high inflation rates over long periods, people can afford fewer things. If they have money saved in interest-free bank accounts, the value of their savings also decreases.

What causes Inflation?

When there is more money available, and the quantity of

goods remains the same, the demand for money will be lower and basic economics will apply. Now, people would be willing to pay more money for the same item, which will cause an increase in the price of that item. An increase in the overall money supply would mean that buyers can pay more for the same things across the board. As a result, there is an increase in the price of items, and the economy will experience inflation. They refer to an imbalance between the money required by an economy for its trade-related needs and the amount of money supplied. It is worth mentioning that an overall sustained increase in prices has to occur for inflation. A singular rise in prices due to demand does not point towards inflation.

Even though most economists agree that an increased money supply is the main reason behind inflation, there are three key drivers of inflation when the supply of money increases.

Demand-Pull Effect

This phenomenon occurs when the population suddenly has a lot more money to spend. Naturally, the demand for items increases. When this demand is unmet by the manufacturers and producers of goods, the demand for goods increases, causing the demand to drive up prices.

Cost-Push Effect

This effect occurs when the demand-pull effect applies to intermediary goods such as oil, utilities, and other raw materials. As the retailers factor in these costs when they price their products, an increase in their price causes an increase in the finished goods' price.

Built-In Inflation

This effect is a result of an economy that has been experiencing inflation for a long time. Employers increase their wages to accommodate the trends. When their wages increase, the cost of labor increases for the producers and manufacturers. This causes an increase in the price of finished goods.

It is important to understand what inflation is. It is not as easily defined as many people might imagine. There are in fact a number of accepted definitions and this can result in misunderstandings, particularly if you start trying to comprehend the economics behind it.

Chapter 1: Inflation and the money supply theory

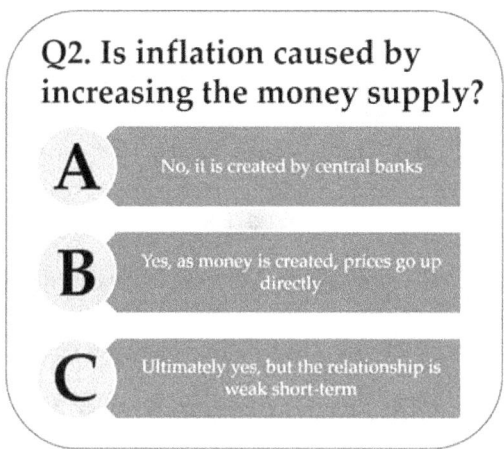

This chapter looks at the most common explanation of inflation i.e. that it is related to the expansion of the money supply. It reviews the evidence for the theory and explains exactly how it is supposed to work.

If you ask most economists what causes inflation, they'll probably mention that it is linked to the amount of money in circulation. As an example, they might ask you to imagine a simple world of bakers and brewers. There might be five bakers and five brewers each selling a loaf and a pint of beer to each other every day. Each costs £1 in gold coins. The total wealth of the world is £10. Now imagine what would happen if another £10 in gold coins is found and everyone gets a share of them.

The amount of money in the world has suddenly doubled to £20 but there are still only 5 loaves and 5 pints of beer being made each day. Everyone feels a bit richer but the only thing they can buy is bread and beer. As people think they have more money, they all try and outbid each other to get extra provisions. Very quickly the prices of all the bread and beer will increase until they cost around £2 and a new equilibrium is reached again. £1 in gold coins now only buys half a loaf or half a pint of beer.

The effect of a money supply increase on prices

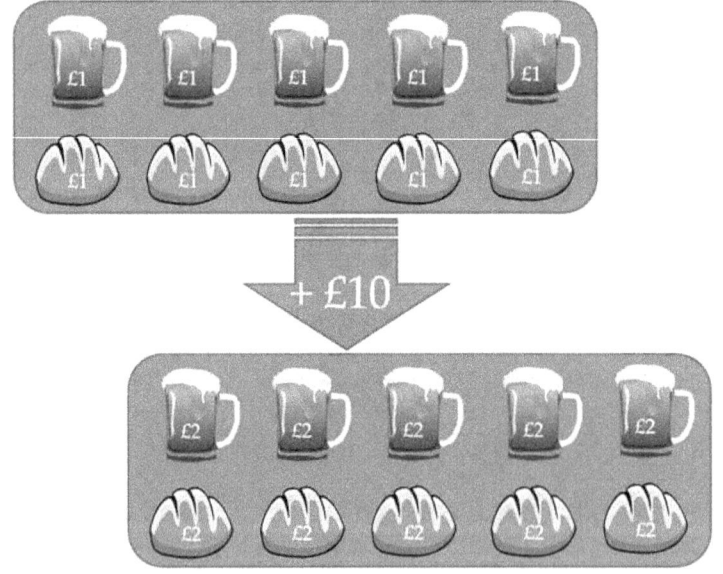

That is a simple example of the theory behind the link between the money supply and inflation. In real life, it is a lot more complex and it can take a long time for prices to rise to the new equilibrium and hence the relationship is not always as visible as the theory suggests it should be. However, there is strong evidence that the theory holds over the medium-term as you'll see below.

History of the theory

Sharp increases in prices have been observed in many periods of ancient history from ancient Babylonia to the Roman Empire. A particularly prolonged period of rising prices throughout the globe was seen in the 16th and early 17th Centuries.

At that time, money was defined in Europe in terms of precious metals. Silver and gold coins were issued as the primary medium of exchange. That era was the time of Christopher Columbus and the great discovery of the Americas. The key thing plundered from the New World and brought back to Europe was vast quantities of gold and silver. This made certain countries and financiers much richer as wealth was defined in terms of precious metals.

The amount of money circulating in Europe therefore increased.

At the same time prices were rising in Europe and many scholars started to suggest reasons why this was happening. Amongst them was the famous astronomer Copernicus. He was one of the first people to propose the theory that the price increases seen were in fact related to the increases in the money supply.

Copernicus - one of the first theorists on Inflation

The key formula

In its most simplified form, scholars such as Copernicus stated that Prices (P) vary in proportion to the supply of money (M) i.e. $P \propto M$.

Quantity theory of money

Many developments and variants of Copernicus's theory have been put forward since. Probably the most notable was in 1848, when John Stewart Mill formally proposed the "quantity theory of money" and produced the "equation of exchange". He showed that the simple formula is only applicable if both the size of the economy is stable (i.e. GDP is constant) and there has been no change in the number of times money is spent during that period by people i.e. people's saving levels and spending levels haven't gone up or down.

The full formula he proposed was thus: MV=PQ.

I will try and translate this jargon into words that might make some more sense. It is saying that at any period of time, the money supply (M) multiplied by the number of times people use that money (V) is equal to the average prices (P) multiplied by the total value of all the goods we produce in that time i.e. GDP (Q).

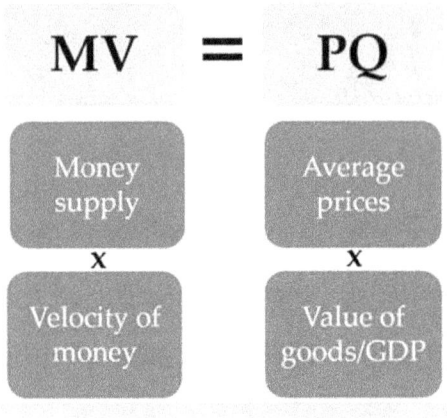

The difficult aspect of this is the number of times people use money, or the "velocity of money", as it is known. This is to do with saving and spending levels. The basic idea behind this qualification is that if lots of people save money, fewer people will be buying goods. For a while at least, too many goods will be being made relative to buyers. Sellers therefore will be forced to drop prices as they compete for what business is left. The reverse situation also occurs when saving decreases and spending levels go up in an economy i.e. prices rise.

Evidence for the theory

Proponents of the theory (called Monetarists) can point to

many more recent examples than the 16th and 17th Centuries where excessive money printing appears directly linked to rising levels of inflation. The most infamous of these was during the Weimar Republic in Germany in the early 1920s. (See: "**8-World War I and learning about hyperinflation**.")

Indeed if you examine the long-term rise in inflation in the UK since 1900, it is strongly correlated to the growth in the money supply. The graph below shows an index of UK prices from 1900 and compares this with an index of the UK money supply. (In order to satisfy the equation of exchange, a deduction from the money supply has been made for the extra money required because of our expanding economy, i.e. the index is money supply less GDP[11].)

The graph shows that over the last century inflation has fairly closely followed the money supply. However there have been quite long periods when one of the two was slightly higher. Indeed for the last couple of decades, consumer price inflation has been lagging behind increases in the money supply in the UK and this situation must be resolved at some point. (See: "**18-The transition period and near-term inflation**".)

The link between UK prices and the money supply

Some issues with the theory

What the above chart also illustrates is that changes in the money supply are not always directly reflected in the prices of goods and services. Indeed the two can go for many years or even decades in opposite directions. This is partly because of changes in people's desire to save/spend (i.e. the velocity of money) and partly because the newly created money does not always flow directly into goods and services - see below.

No one tells the population that the money supply has increased. The very first response to an increase in money supply is often for people to save, and so effectively they keep the amount of money in circulation the same. Therefore prices do not immediately change either. As that money spreads further around the economy, more and more gets into circulation. Prices then rise. Furthermore, money supply and velocity of money are often correlated. As money supply increases, velocity of money goes up (and vice versa in a recession) and so the price changes can be bigger than the money supply calculations alone might predict.

To further complicate matters, this process is very much dependent on where the increases in money supply have gone (i.e. into retail prices or into asset prices) and more generally on consumer sentiment and the state of the business climate and cycle. It is therefore not surprising that there is often little short-term synchronicity between the money supply and inflation. This is clearly illustrated in the data from the UK in recent years.

There has been little correlation between the money supply and inflation in the last 20 years

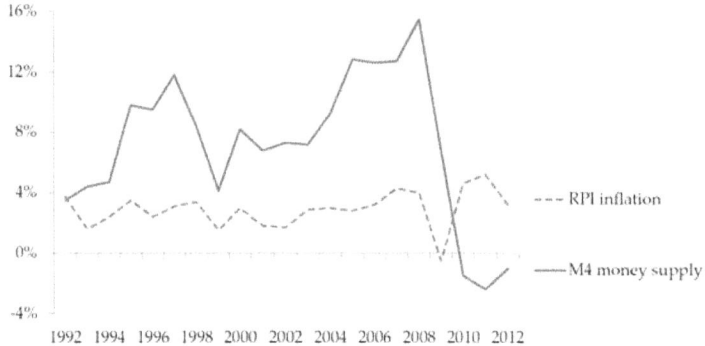

Sources: Bank of England, 12-month change in money supply M4 and ONS annual RPI inflation.

As the above chart shows, there has been little correlation between increases in the money supply in the UK and retail inflation in the twenty years between 1992 and 2012.

Many economists now acknowledge that changes in the money supply are not predictive of retail inflation over short-term periods or in low-inflation environments. In a recent paper examining the real world correlation between money supply and inflation of all countries between 1969 and 1999, the following conclusion was reached:

"This strong link between inflation and money growth is almost wholly due to the presence of high-inflation or hyperinflation countries in the sample. The relation between inflation and money growth for low-inflation countries (on average less than 10 per cent per year over 30 years) is weak, if not absent."

Money supply and asset price inflation

But what these simplistic analyses of monetary theory miss out is the complexity of inflation. To comprehend this, you need to understand exactly how the money supply is expanded. Money is normally created in an economy when private banks make loans to individuals or companies. (See box below: "How money is created.") Typically this money is first used for speculation or to purchase assets e.g. houses, companies/shares, bonds, commodities (or more complex derivatives of them). It is not normally created to spend directly in the economy on goods and services, although typically it ends up there.

Therefore when the money supply is expanded, as happened markedly during the 80s and the following decades in the UK, it creates inflation in the assets that the money is first used for. This so-called "asset price inflation" is clearly illustrated in the chart below with data from the UK.

Asset price inflation and the money supply

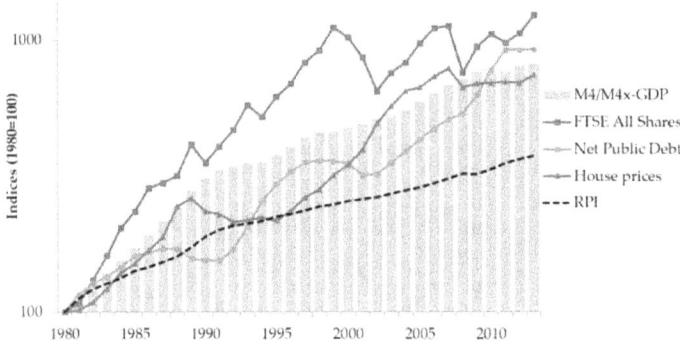

Sources: Price index - ONS longitudinal series. Money supply - **Bank of England** (M3/M4/M4x). GDP - measuringworth.com. FTSE - Finfacts and SwallowPark. Net Public Debt - ukpublicspending.co.uk . House prices - ONS.

The solid bars on the chart show an index of the money supply (M4/M4x) less GDP growth, i.e. the net increase in the money supply over and above that required by the UK economy during this time. The lines show where that money then flowed to. These depict the index prices of key asset classes such as shares (i.e. FTSE All Share Index), bonds (i.e. Net Public Debt) and house prices. It shows that a series of bubbles were created over this period in these assets. The prices of all of them have kept up with or exceeded the overall increase in the money supply.

The dotted line on the chart shows an index of goods and services prices (RPI) and how the expanded money supply since 1980 has yet to have its full impact in this area.

Two separate money supplies? Two separate inflations?

What is key to understand about the quantity theory of money concerning inflation and the money supply is that it affects two separate economies: wealth (i.e. asset prices) and consumer spending (i.e. goods and service prices). Money flows between these two economies. For example when someone sells a house and spends the proceeds in the real economy on goods/services like holidays or health care, they are transferring money from one economy to the other. Similarly when they save their salary in a pension, money is transferred in the opposite direction.

It has been argued that the two sectors obey the quantity theory separately (and over the medium-term in totality too). However economists rarely highlight this issue. This is probably because it is difficult to demonstrate as countries do not normally publish data separately for the money supply in the two areas.

Chapter 2: China Dominating The New World Order since 2016

Why is the Economy of China Growing so Fast?

Around 1997 when Great Britain's hundred year lease on Hong Kong expired and they returned it to China, something happened to the Chinese government. Maybe they saw the potential to massively grow their own economy with the addition of the huge economy of Hong Kong.

The communist leadership decided that they should allow the people additional economic freedom. They permitted more capitalism and opened up increasingly free markets. With around a billion and a half citizens now encouraged to work harder to make something for themselves, their economy began to grow rapidly.

Besides this, the Chinese followed two other approaches to vault their economy ahead. They aggressively pursued a policy of stealing technology, patents, and secrets from companies throughout the West. At the same time, they invested the currency that their growing exports earned in overseas corporations and valuable resources on every continent. This has spurred their economic growth and helped to fuel their unprecedented expansion that has raged along at often eleven percent GDP growth per year.

Another thing that the Chinese have done to expand their economy rapidly is to artificially hold down the value of their currency the Yuan. They do not allow the exchange rate to float freely on international markets.

This keeps their exports cheap versus industrial rivals like the US, Japan, Great Britain, and the European Union countries. Through all of these efforts, the Chinese have managed to achieve growth rates not seen in the economically more mature West in around a hundred years.

What are the Consequences for the US?

MarketWatch claims that the date of 2016 when China passes the U.S. economically is a watershed event for the United States. They have called the forecast from the IMF a bombshell that will mark the conclusion of the Age of America. Besides this, they claim that it will be a dark cloud for the U.S. dollar and its huge treasury market.

Newspapers in the United Kingdom have gone further. The Daily Mail claims that the consequences for the U.S. will be a loss of dominant world power status. They even stated that the president who is elected in 2012 will be caretaker for the decline and fall of the U.S.

The Chinese already hold the U.S. hostage today. They have as much as three trillion worth of U.S. dollar holdings that they could begin to dump at any point that it suited them. This would crush the U.S. ability to finance its enormous debts and spending along with the value of the dollar. It would cause damage to the U.S. economy and dollar that would probably never be repaired.

Some analysts claim that this transition of power will lead to a new world order that is run by a handful of power brokers including China's communist leadership. Billionaire currency investor George Soros is one who believes this will come to pass.

This would not be good news for people of the world, as the Chinese government continues to display its brutality and indifference to human life. This stands in marked contrast to the values of liberty, human and property rights, and free markets that both the U.S. and Great Britain before it have embraced and spread around the world.

What will Happen to the Dollar as the World's Reserve Currency?

There is already a lot of quiet discussion on the world that will emerge after the dollar is no longer the reserve currency. The French, Chinese, Russians, and Gulf Oil States have held secret meetings about alternative reserve currencies that the U.S. did not even receive advance notice of or an invitation to attend. Perhaps the last transfer of world reserve currency status is a good example to examine.

The British Empire's economy ceased to be the largest in the world in the early years of the 1900's as America's economy gained ground and overtook it. Yet the pound remained the reserve currency for the world until the end of two world wars, almost fifty years later. This might give the U.S some more time. Do you think the transition from U.S. Dollar to some other reserve currency will take as long?

The Most Valuable Financial Secret In The World

Everyone would like to know the most valuable financial secret in the world. The revelation of this mystery may come as a shock to you. Gold represents the past, present, and future store of value against which all other goods and even currencies have been and will again be measured.

If you can take advantage of this unshakable truth now, then you will profit hugely when the U.S. and other Western nations return to the gold standard in the next decade. In the paragraphs that follow, you will understand why the gold standard has been historically critical, why gold is a timeless store of value that prevents credit and financial collapse, hyperinflation, and currency devaluation, and why the West will soon seek to return to the shelter of its protecting power in only a few short years.

Why Is The Gold Standard So Important?

With a gold standard that backs up a currency, the currency is literally as good as gold. It can only be issued in amounts that correlate with the fixed gold stocks in a nation's vaults.

This is why individuals who are in favor of greater roles of free markets, higher levels of individual responsibility and freedom, and a restriction on government power love money that is backed by gold instead of mere faith and trust in unreliable governments. You simply cannot print gold or manipulate its tangible supply, no matter how powerful your government is.

History and Effectiveness of the Modern Age Gold Standard

It may come as a shock to you that for most of their history, the U.S. and Great Britain possessed banking and currency systems that were backed up by gold. Beginning in 1750, the government of King George made it illegal to issue paper money.

The American economy then began to run on silver Spanish pieces of eight and gold coins for bank reserves. This gold standard governed the U.S. and British systems more or less from the years 1750 and 1971.

How well did such a system function? All the way up until President Franklin D. Roosevelt chose to intentionally devalue the dollar in 1933 when he seized control of all gold in the nation, the costs of goods and services remained incredibly stable.

The U.S. dollar's purchasing power remained almost constant over nearly two hundred years. Would that this were the case today, instead of the dollar dropping by fifty percent over the last decade and by a shocking over ninety-seven percent since 1971.

Timeless Store of Value Provides Immunity to Financial Busts

The main reason that gold functions as the greatest financial asset in the world is that it has always maintained its purchasing power throughout all known history. For thousands of years, gold has remained a timeless and globally accepted store of value.

The yellow metal is extraordinarily suited to be a currency after all, since it is rare, divisible, portable, and enduring. To give you an example of how well gold maintains your purchasing power, consider that one hundred years ago a twenty dollar gold piece bought a fine hand crafted suit.

Today, the same twenty dollar gold piece will buy you a fine luxury Italian suit.

The great advantage to your currency being backed by this timeless store of value lies in the stability that it provides. Money systems that are backed up by gold are practically impervious to major destabilizing economic boom and bust cycles. This results from the fact that the money and credit supplies are both rigorously regulated by the value of a nation's economy.

A bigger economy translates to more gold, which allows for a larger amount of credit and currency to be extended. This means that the insatiable greed of bankers is not allowed to play havoc with a nation's economy, since they can only make loans out of money based on their tangible gold reserves.

No Way to Protect Savings from Inflation Without Gold Standard

Alan Greenspan once famously wrote that in the absence of the gold standard, you could not keep savings from being diminished by inflation. Money is not a secure store of value without it.

Your savings can be safeguarded against inflation when the currency is backed up by gold.

While there may be other ways to protect the value of your money, such as when you purchase real estate or high quality stocks, there is no better way to protect yourself with liquid and portable real money than with gold.

Excessive Debt Burden Leads to Hyperinflation or Default

Without the gold standard, a nation's debts are allowed to rise to perilous and even unthinkable levels. This is not possible with the gold standard. It is simply a function of the quantity of the country's gold reserves restricting the amount of debt that the nation is able to carry. Bank reserves can only expand in tandem with the size of the economy, which prevents banks from taking on heavy debt loads as well.

Once President Nixon took the U.S. and most of the world off of the gold standard with his actions in 1971, creditors lost their legal rights to the country's gold reserves. At this point, the banks no longer had any limitations to their powers to create new money and credit from thin air, except for the Federal Reserve and its ratios.

The Debt Load Began To Explode

Within years, the debt load began to explode in the U.S. and developed world. The banking system expanded astronomically, since it no longer had to acquire additional gold reserves from greater trade or industrial expansion.

When you consider the actual debt of the U.S. to include unfunded entitlements, the American public debt amounts to a shocking **fifty-six trillion dollars**. This is nearly four times the size of the country's Gross Domestic Product, or annual total of all goods and services produced in the nation. It also translates to almost seven hundred thousand dollars of debt for every family in the U.S.

These debts cannot ever be paid back in today's dollars. This leaves only a few solutions for Western governments that are increasingly desperate. They can default on the debt, which causes the whole economy to fall apart.

Alternatively, they can devalue away the unsustainable debts through currency devaluation and the hyperinflation that inevitably results.

One way to do this is to print literally trillions of new dollars. This has been going on at the Federal Reserve since 2007, and it continues unabated today. One day, this will cause the value of the U.S. dollar to collapse. This in turn will lead to runaway hyperinflation, where the prices of goods and services rise from ten to hundreds of percent each month or year.

Once the U.S. money system falls apart because of all of the unchecked debt and money printing that the departure from the gold standard permitted, politicians will finally look at options for what has to replace the fiat paper U.S. dollar.

Is the Gold Standard Still Practical Today?

There will be many pundits, bankers, and politicians who try to convince you and the public that a return to the gold standard is a terrible idea. The reason that bank and government officials will fight the return of gold backed money with all of their collective strength is simple.

Under the rules of the gold backed currency, they will lose most of their incredible power. Money will no longer be created from thin air with the push of a computer button. The money supply will no longer be micro-manageable.

- **The government will have to live within its means more or less.**

Is it practical to talk about a return to the gold standard? The nation has two hundred and sixty-three million troy ounces of gold. With a two trillion dollar money base in dollars, you divide the number of dollars by the nation's gold supply to come up with a gold price of $7,604 per ounce to convert to a currency that is completely backed up by gold.

Is there a living example left for how the gold stand works out nowadays? Switzerland never abandoned the gold standard. The Swiss Franc is still backed up by gold, according to their constitution, to this day. You be the judge. How has their economic stability turned out over the last forty years?

Save Your Financial Assets From The Gathering Storm

If you listen to the financial media much, then you have no doubt heard the almost passionate claims that the U.S. and world economies have recovered from the brink of the disaster that was the financial crisis and Great Recession. Your own personal experiences may tell you otherwise.

Have you ever wondered if the talking heads and politicians are telling you a lie in order to attempt to hold the world economy together as long as possible? The new book "Debt, Deficits, and the Demise of the American Economy" argues the case that the next and by far worst stage of the global economic catastrophe is set to unfold in the future and has already begun.

About the Authors Jeff Cox and Peter J. Tanous

Jeff Cox and Peter J. Tanous wrote this new work "Debt, Deficits, and the Demise of the American Economy" after sharing conversations last year on where the global economy is headed. Jeff Cox is a staff writer for CNBC.com, the financial channel. He has worked as a journalist since 1987. His regular appearances on CNBC

TV showcase his market commentaries. Cox's articles are regularly featured on such well known financial sites as Yahoo!, TheStreet.com, and AOL Money.

Co-author Peter Tanous is the President of investment advisory firm Lepercq Lynx. He has worked in the capacity of financial adviser professional for more than forty years. He co-established international investment bank Petra Capital Corporation. Tanous also served as vice president and later international regional director for Smith Barney. Peter Tanous has written a few well regarded books like Investment Gurus and The Wealth Equation.

What is the Premise of the Book?

The bad news is that you have been sold a cruel deception with this idea that the global and U.S. economies are in the midst of a vibrant recovery since 2009. As recently as last August, Alan Greenspan, long time chairman of the Federal Reserve, stated that we now face the dilemma of the most extraordinary financial crisis that he has either read about or personally witnessed. He made this statement a full year after the Great Recession and financial crisis were supposed to have ended.

"Debt, Deficits, and the Demise of the American Economy" picks up with this sobering claim by Alan Greenspan and then takes you the reader on a linear and logical tour of how this crisis happened in the first place and where it is all headed in the bitter end. They call this the most severe financial disaster in all of American history.

The Euro Devaluation Will Continue

The next stages of the financial Armageddon are already beginning today. This involves the utter collapse of the European peripheral countries, which will begin with Greece and next Ireland. The resulting confidence crisis in banks throughout Europe will cause a serious Euro devaluation. You may say that sounds bad for our friends in Europe, but how does it impact the U.S. on a direct level?

As a result of this tragedy in the Eurozone, panic will next break out in stock markets around the world. The violent fear and continuous uncertainty will cause a severe and fast sell off in the global stock exchanges. Then the world bond markets will practically cease to operate and this will cause the interest rates around the globe to soar.

This is when the spotlight will turn to the U.S. Because of the astronomical debt level and runaway deficit spending that we have engaged in here, the panic will spread to the American shores. The Treasury will attempt to pay the debts with freshly printed hundreds of billions of dollars.

As the financial situation declines in the States, investors in the critical U.S. Treasuries markets will lose their necessary confidence to keep buying the U.S. debt. Interest rates in the country will spike. This will lead to a default of a number of states on their municipal debts.

Retirement Payments Will Stop

State offices will also stop sending out retirement payments to the retired state employees. After these events occur, one thing after another will cascade until roaring inflation takes hold on a level not seen in modern America.

This gruesome and depressing situation may sound impossible or at least unlikely to you now. Once you read this work and learn about the present state of the global financial system, it will not anymore. Authors Cox and Tanous show you that the nonsense being spouted by

Washington and New York flies in the face of the cold hard reality.

The final conclusion is a sober one, that the day of reckoning for the years of out of control Federal government spending is about to come due. The book says that we have already walked too far down the road of destruction to even contemplate turning around and retracing our misguided steps. The authors are convinced that a collapse of the global economy will inexorably result.

What Has Caused the Problems?

The authors are certain that the dangers posed by sovereign nations' enormous debts have been grossly underestimated. The U.S. is not immune from this in the least. The fourteen trillion dollar U.S. debt will have to be paid eventually, one way or the other. This puts the world squarely on a crash course with hyperinflation the likes that the country has never personally experienced before.

What Does the Book Predict?

"Debt, Deficits, and the Demise of the American

Economy" says that events have already gone too far for us to avoid this next stage of the still unfolding crisis. The authors say that the resulting financial calamity will prove to be worse than what you saw when the financial system collapsed in 2008 to 2009.

First the Euro will collapse, and next the house of cards that is the U.S. debt will fall. In the wake of these twin events, U.S. and world markets will be paralyzed and crushed. They claim that this will happen with the stock market crashing in 2012 or even this very year. There will be runs on all of the banks and an amount of inflation which almost no one is expecting.

What Can You Do to Protect Yourself Personally?

The book does not leave you without solutions. The events that are to come may be unavoidable now, but there is still ample time to protect your finances until the vicious storm finally passes. The authors point out that the traditional allocations in to stocks and bonds will not save you. Instead, you will need to have a major stake in the tested inflation proof assets like gold, silver, oil, timber, and farmland, along with bonds that are inflation protected.

Verdict of the Book

Jeff Cox and Peter Tanous set out to write a book that the person on the street without an economics degree or background could understand. They have succeeded in their efforts to pen the story of how we got here, what the price to pay will be, and how you can save your financial assets from the gathering storm.

The authors expressly state that they do not want to engage in the spread of fear. Instead, they want you the reader to understand what the real bills are that will shortly have to be paid for the extravagance of the last ten years. They believe that foreknowledge allows you to be prepared.

If you want to protect your hard earned money from the ravages of U.S. debt collapse and hyperinflation, then you had best read "Debt, Deficits, and the Demise of the American Economy" and take quick action. The authors provide you with sound strategies for your investments.

They also offer the U.S. government a detailed plan for how to pull the country out of the economic catastrophe once it happens. This makes it required reading for you and your government officials as you prepare for and deal with the global depression that is soon to rear its ugly head.

What could be worse than hearing "I told you so" tomorrow if you have done nothing to protect yourself today?

E-Inflation

Have you ever wondered why the price of the things you are used to buying keeps increasing? Have you ever wondered why would a state of the art Ford Mustang in the 60s be worth 2000$ whereas it is worth more than 27,000$ today? Or better yet, have you ever contemplated your grandparents' tales of how they would go through the whole day with a single nickel? If yes, then allow me to introduce you to the mysterious phenomenon known as inflation. Inflation is the consistent increase in the prices of goods and services produced within a country. In other words, the inflation is the amount by which the value of your money decreases. Inflation is calculated using a tool called the CPI (Consumer Price Index) which examines the price of certain commodities (Called basket) and how they change over time. Now let us try to calculate inflation to better grasp what it implies

Suppose an economy that consumes nothing but apples, bananas and oranges.

Now, suppose we form a basket with the quantities we consume of each, and their price to determine how much did they cost a year ago

1 Apple * 1(the price of apples a year ago)=1$

1 Banana* 2=2$

1 Orange*3=3$

Total price of basket=6$

Now, let us calculate the price of the same basket using today's (hypothetical) Prices

1 Apple*1.5=1.5$

1 Banana*3=3$

1 Orange*4.5=4.5$

Total price of basket in today's prices=9$

And as such, inflation is calculated. It now costs 9$ to buy the same things that used to cost 6$. (9-6)/6 yield 50%, and that is what is called the inflation rate. So, in the above example, this is an economy where money loses its value by 50% each year. Inflation is a headache to any government, because it influences all other factors in the economy. For instance, relying on the above example, no single investor would be attracted to invest in a country whose currency is losing half of its value every single year. The inflation rate captures this decrease in the purchasing power as a percentage rate. It is worth mentioning that inflation is a very serious economic phenomenon that every country pays attention to, and it is characteristic of a healthy economy and a developed country to have a low inflation rate. Inflation is usually caused by one of two reasons. First, the consumers go on a shopping mania, buying everything therefore increasing the prices of goods, leading to inflation. Second reason comes from the other side, that of the supplier, when they choose to keep most of the goods that they own, therefore selling much fewer amounts whereas the demand is the same, which will eventually also leads to inflation

I hope that you had fully grasped the concept of inflation,

how it calculated and how it affects every single person in the economy. Inflation rate is a very good indicator of the efficiency with which the government is running the country's economy. Please, check Egypt's inflation rates if you want to have a feel of how it is like living in a country run by financially irresponsible leaders.

F- GDP (Gross Domestic Product)

If a single factor was to be chosen as the single, most important, one of all, it would be the GDP. Gross Domestic Product is the market value of all the goods and services produced within a country in a given period of time (Annually, quarterly, or monthly). What that means is, it is the value of the total goods and services that this country was able to produce within the specified time period. What makes GDP very important is that it is the single factor that encompasses all other factors, since it is the number the can mirror the whole of the economy. The economic objective of any government is to increase its country GDP while controlling all other factors such as inflation, interest rates and exchange rates.

G-Interest Rate

The interest rate is the rate which an investor should expect to receive if he decides to place his money in a bank. The interest rate is usually seen as the percentage of extra gain that one should expect, because he took the risk of investing and because of lending some money which he could have used to fulfill his personal needs. This is one of the key components of any economy as it has a major effect on all of its parts. To fully understand interest rate and its effect, one must understand its second definition and use. The interest rate represents a different factor for the person who wants to borrow money. As opposite to the lender, the interest rate to the borrower represents the extra cost that he must pays in order to acquire a certain sum of money. The interest rate is mainly controlled, maintained and changed by the country's central bank.

H-Unemployment

Another economic indicator that is ought to be explained is the amount of unemployed people in a country, measured by the unemployment rate. An unemployed person is defined as one who: Is within the working age (above 16 and below 60), has no disability that would stop him from working (mental or physical), and finally is actively seeking a job. If a person fits the three criteria, then he is considered unemployed. Unemployment is very serious because it is considered a problem economically and socially. For instance, countries with higher unemployment rate often have higher rates of crime. Unemployment is present in the most solid of economies, no single economy has 100% employment rate. Economists estimate that there must be at least 5% of the labor force that is unemployed. The reasons why unemployment cannot be completely eradicated stems from its different types that are to be covered momentarily.

There are four types of unemployment: Frictional, structural, seasonal and cyclical.

Frictional unemployment is the normal type of unemployment; it happens as a result of people changing jobs, there are always people who are looking to change their jobs. Also, people who are taking a break from their job for whatever reasons are categorized under frictional unemployment.

Structural unemployment is one that results from the

world having developed newer technologies. Consider people who used to sell VCR tapes, in the age of Netflix, this once flourishing technology has declined over the years due to the advancement in the technology. The people who used to manufacture VCRs or sell VCR tapes are now left to find another job.

Seasonal unemployment is, as the name suggests, the one that occurs due changes in the weather. For instance, the tourism market in Egypt flourishes in summer, whereas people working in this sector usually can find better things to do when winter comes, since there is no touristic demand on Egypt in its winter

Cyclical unemployment is the most important one of all four. It is the unemployment that results from the country's economy having greatly declined, which results in lots of people losing their jobs, as happened in the US. Following the 2008 financial crisis

Money Supply

The money supply is defined as all the liquid currency inside of an economy, it is the total amount of cash, coins and saving bank accounts held by its citizens. Money supply is an important part of any economy, the reason money supply needs to be monitored is because it cannot exist in excess or scarcity, both states have negative economic consequences. Money supply always needs to be at the right amount, no more and no less, that's why it is heavily monitored and regulated.

Fiscal Policy and Monetary Policy

I certainly hope by now that you have understood how stupendous a country's economy is. With such size and complexity, things are ought to be controlled in order not to go out of hand. The entity that is responsible for managing a country's economy is it government, and they manage it using both its fiscal and monetary policy.

The monetary policy of a country is one that is most primarily concerned with deciding its interest rate and money supply, both of which have an immense outcome on its economy.

The fiscal policy of a country is one that is concerned with how much should the government tax its people, and how it should spend the money it had acquired through these taxes

Chapter 3: Price stability and the consolidation period

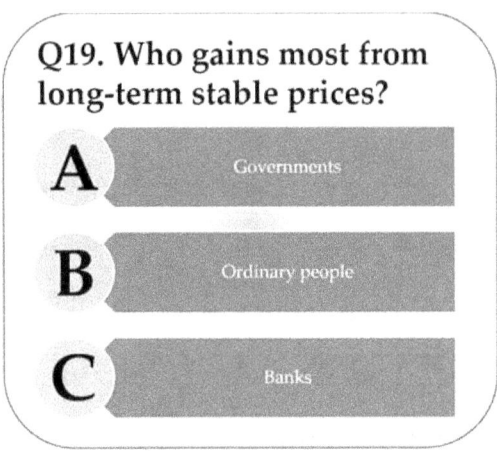

Following the transition phase, there could follow a period of relatively stable prices that could take the world into the 22nd Century. This could well be facilitated by major changes in the monetary system which would help maintain this stability. It would not mean that prices remain static. Instead over time and in aggregate they would stay around the same level and slightly decline due to technological and efficiency improvements.

There would be major implications for workers, who would be incentivized to improve productivity to gain a pay rise. The value of real wages would increase and this would be supported by the slight decline in prices overall. Inequality would therefore reduce. Business (though probably not the finance industry) would prosper. Governments would need to find new sources of taxation to replace the loss of inflation tax. Finally, increasing global prosperity in the late 21st Century might well lead to a rise in the population and a new inflationary wave would begin all over again.

A new monetary system: Chicago or bust

The transition period to the consolidation wave is likely to be a turbulent one for world finances. We've seen that historically the transition is often associated with some form of calamity and accompanied by prices declining by a half temporarily. Such an event, like the bond crisis scenario example, is likely to be accompanied by public demand for complete reform of the banking and monetary system to ensure such episodes do not happen again. In addition, there may be such distrust of the existing financial order that any new innovations that appear to solve the problems would be examined very seriously.

A similar situation occurred in the 1930s and resulted in proposals such as the Chicago Plan. This sought to reform the banking system. A body was to be created to monitor the money supply and create just enough to cover the natural growth of the economy, thereby largely eliminating the boom and bust cycle. By definition, such a stable monetary world would have near-zero inflation over the long-term.

As we have seen, governments after World War II decided on a different policy of persistent inflation and the Chicago Plan was rejected. However the potential scale of the crisis this time could be so much larger than the 1930s and could affect so many people in so many countries that reform of some sort would be a very likely outcome. The format of that reform is impossible to predict. Its objective though might be to create a world where debt cannot spiral out of control for the benefit of certain individuals. A new trusted monetary system would be required that is transparent and independent of the influence of individuals, companies or governments.

The blockchain world

One such solution to these new demands might be based on "blockchain", the technology behind digital currencies like Bitcoin. The essence of this is that a public and transparent record is kept of all transactions that take place. The amount of money created would be regulated by some agreed formula and therefore not be open to easy abuse by individuals or governments. Concepts such as leverage, debt and derivatives do not exist with so-called cryptocurrencies based on block chain.

An existing cryptocurrency like Bitcoin is unlikely to be suitable for long-term global adoption. This is because Bitcoin was designed to have an increase in money supply over a period of just 20 years and that increase was linked to the speed of machines to mine bitcoins rather than being related to economic needs for money within an economy. It also has had unfortunate associations with asset bubbles and the criminal underworld.

However the technology behind it does have potential and could be used to facilitate a new monetary system for the world. This is because it could create a monetary system that complies with Marcks's three criteria for stopping inflation. (See: "**18-The transition period and near-term inflation.**") These are:

1. **It could provide a process to regulate and stop net money supply from rising.**
2. **It would encourage stable prices (as the value of money would not change) and so latent inflation could not build up.**
3. **Inventing money by borrowing would not be possible and so levels of debt would not increase again to unsustainable levels.**

Inflation would never disappear

It is very important to understand that there would not be zero inflation in the consolidation wave. Periodic changes would never disappear, possibly as an effect of wars, shortages, commodity price rises or exchange rate changes. The Keynesian ideas of cost-pull and demand-push inflation would still have an impact on short-term inflation rates, as they always have. What would be different is that in most cases, after prices rises, overall prices would eventually decline back to their original levels as there would have been no change in the net money supply.

The prices of the individual 600+ items in a typical price index would also vary, sometimes substantially. The effects of supply and demand would not be extinguished and some items might consistently increase in price because of this. However there would be an overall drag of lower levels of prices from many items as the impact of technology or productivity improvements reduced their cost of production. In the digital world in which we increasingly live, the cost of producing many things is trending towards zero and the full impact of this would become more apparent. 3D printing for example could have a massive impact on the world economy when the technology fully evolves, possibly as much as the internet has had over recent decades.

A final key factor is that we are talking here about average global inflation. There may still be a few countries that decide to organize themselves by increasing their money supply and printing money. Inflation would inevitably ensue. However it is likely that structural changes to the new financial order would make this more difficult and their overall impact on world inflation would be minimal. Remember there were no instances of hyperinflation anywhere in the world during the last three consolidation phases.

Implications for pay and inequality

One of the key effects of the consolidation wave would be to instill in the world a different outlook with regard to inflation. Annual wage rises would become a distant memory. Instead workers would only get wage increases when they became more skilled or improved their productivity. Moreover the value of different jobs would become clearer as people came to know the rates over time and the picture was no longer confused by the impact of inflation.

Reasons inequality would decline

- Incentive to improve wages through higher productivity or reskilling/moving job
- Gradually lower prices for goods increasing purchasing power
- Wealth destruction during transition phase

The most likely effect of this change in attitude would be to act as a strong incentive for people to increase their wages either by improving their output in their current job or by reskilling to get a different more highly-paid job. Over time, people would be able to clearly see the effect of the changes they have made themselves on their salary and this should create a positive feedback loop. Contrast this to the current system, where most people receive annual pay rises whether they are doing a good job or not. Moreover evidence shows that they erroneously attribute these rises to their own skill and not to inflation.

Combine this effect of slightly rising average wages with the overall gradual decline in prices of goods and services and the net spending power of the bulk of the population would rise. Inequality would therefore decline as it has done before in the consolidation wave. This would be reinforced by the fact that the wealthy would be unlikely to see the massive asset price gains they have seen over recent decades. Tight controls on the money supply would stop them. Moreover the rich would have more than likely suffered a sharp decline in their wealth during the transition period, which would already have levelled the inequality field significantly.

Implications for business

Contrary to the established dogma that business needs the subsidy of stealth inflation tax to survive, I believe the overall impact on business would be positive once we are through the transition period. There is a number of reasons for this.

Reasons business would flourish

- More stable economic environment
- More transparency in sales and profits
- Better decision making
- Less "shoe leather" costs
- Less competition from zombie companies
- More investment and less share buy backs

One of the key implications of near-zero inflation would be decreased costs for business because of the removal of the need to constantly change prices. Such "shoe leather" costs, as economists sometimes refer to them, mean that companies divert time and energy away from more productive activity. The removal of inflation as a variable from a company's sales also makes it much easier for stakeholders (both management and shareholders) to truly see what is happening to a business. For example food-price deflation recently in the UK has clearly exposed the lack of growth in major food retailers that was not obvious before.

In his book**, Less Than Zero**, Professor George Selgin put forward a number of arguments why a zero-inflation world would be better for business. He thinks it would lead to greater macroeconomic stability with fewer booms and busts. He also thinks it would allow for prices and wages to change only in industries where there has been a change in productivity or costs. He also argues that businesses would make better decisions.

The other overriding impact on business would come from different credit conditions brought about by changes to the monetary system. The reduced credit facilities likely to result from removing banks' privilege to invent money would have a major impact. Far fewer companies would be able to massage their apparent profitability by leverage and schemes such as share buy backs. This would encourage companies instead to invest in an attempt to create genuine growth.

The cost of funding would also return to levels where there is a reasonable risk premium. This would discourage zombie companies and create a climate for more innovative new companies to evolve. Funding sources would also change and this would have implications for business. There is likely to be increased crowdfunding of new companies (that is, funding from retail investors) and funding by venture capitalists (funding from high net worth investors). Such investors are likely to seek greater transparency, which might lead to greater efficiency and more profitable companies.

A key difference to the current world would be that the financial sector would be much smaller. A combination of wealth destruction during the transition phase, regulation and a new monetary system would all significantly reduce the size of the global financial market. It would primarily be just an administrative function with regard to money. Investment banks would still exist but their ability to create opaque derivatives might well be more restrained, especially if the next major financial crisis was made worse by them.

Chapter 4: The Strategies Employed in Forex Trading

Forex trading is not as complex as you think it is. In fact, it is quite easy if you know what to do.

Fundamental analysis

Now those of you that are stock market experts will be aware of the fundamental and technical analysis that is conducted on stocks. It involves looking at the company's background, calculating the P/E ratio, calculating the return on investment ratio, etc. All of these are calculated to check whether a particular stock is undervalued and to quickly invest in it.

But this system only works in the stock market and not the forex market. The fundamental analysis that is conducted in the forex market is much different. Although they are both known as fundamental analysis, they take into consideration different factors.

In the forex market, the fundamental analysis refers to studying the economic conditions that prevail in the individual countries in order to understand their impact on currency fluctuations. Let us look at some of the factors that you have to understand in detail if you wish to conduct this type of analysis on the currencies.

Interest rates

The very first factor that influences the currency rates is the interest rates. The interest rates that prevail in a particular country are always controlled by the country's central bank. The interest rates control the currency values to a very large extent. In fact, it has been observed that mere rumors of changes in the interest rates have generated a lot of movement in the forex markets. The two are that closely knit and go hand in hand. So, in order to know whether or not the rates will be affected by the economic makeup of a country, you have to keep an eye on the interest rates.

Employment

The employment scenario of a country determines the value of the local currency. As you know, if a person is employed then he or she will have the power to buy more. This will impact the value of the currency. It ends up affecting inflation, and this will cause the value of the currency to rise. For this, you have to look at the number of employed and number of unemployed people. If the employed is more than the unemployed, then the prices will be stable. But if there is a wave of layoffs then the value of the currency will be affected.

GDP

GDP refers to the gross domestic product. Gross domestic product refers to how much the nation is earning collectively. This includes per capita income and also the consumer price index. You have to study these two factors of a company if you wish to understand how much they are earning and how it will affect the value of the currency. Some countries think of it as a good thing for the GDP to rise, as it will indicate the economic stability that prevails in the country. However, if the GDP rises then it also means that the value of the goods in the country is rising which makes it a bad thing for the economy of the country.

Prices of commodities

The prices of commodities will have a direct bearing on the country's currency value. You have to look at the prices that basic goods are sold at. They will help you determine whether or not the value of the currency will remain stable or fluctuate. You have to read the news regularly and see if there is any movement in the prices of these commodities. If so, is there news of it affecting the economic situation in the country? These are the questions that will have to be asked and answered to arrive at the answer.

Weather conditions

Sometimes, extreme weather conditions or natural calamities also have an impact on the rate of the currency. You have to watch the news to know about these and see if they really are impacting the value of the country's currency.

These form the different things that you should look into to see if the value of a particular country's currency would rise or fall.

Technical analysis

The technical analysis of forex deals with indulging in some heavy-duty mathematics and statistics. It is comparable to the approach that is taken towards calculating the technical analysis related to the stock market. There are a few complex equations that you should calculate, and they are discussed as under.

Moving averages

Moving averages refer to using the power of the trend to assess the direction of the market. As you know, it is extremely important for you to be able to predict how the value of the currency will move next. For this, it is best to go through the different trends that the value of the currency has been following in the recent past. The basic idea is to trace the trend that the price has been following. How is it moving ahead, where does the price reversal point lie, at what point is it most profitable to sell the currency, etc.?

There are three main types of moving averages namely the simple moving average, the weighted moving average and the exponential moving average. The simple moving average method is the easiest one. You have to take a series of price points, add them all together and then divide them by the total number of price points. This is a very basic method yet quite effective. The next type is the weighted moving average method. In this method, you assign the rates numbers based on the time when they were calculated. The oldest one receives 1 and so on. The third method is the exponential moving average method and involves extreme mathematical calculations, which goes beyond the scope of this book.

Bollinger bands

Bollinger bands are the next technical analysis that you must run your currency pair through. This type was developed by John Bollinger. It involves understanding the real-time volatility that a pair of currencies will go through. Just like the moving averages, here too, there are certain situations where you have to employ this technique to arrive at the appropriate results. For example, you have to use at the standard deviations as a tool to measure the pattern of fluctuations in the currency pair. Similarly, you have to use other statistical tools and use it in relation to the Bollinger bands to arrive at a particular trend.

Relative strength index

The relative strength index is a great statistical tool that you can use to check whether a currency is valued at the right price or over or under valued. It is important for you to check this, as you need to buy a currency that is valued at the right price. Once you apply this technique on the trend of the currency, you will find a number. If the number is 30 or under then the currency is oversold, and if it is 70 or higher then it means that it is overbought. Both of these can be a bad thing for any currency. So you have to steer clear off of them and look for pairs that lie in between. The calculation of RSI is generally seen as a tedious task. But the good news is that there are many software available that will easily and quickly calculate the amount for you without having to put in too much effort towards.

Stochastic oscillator

The stochastic oscillator is a system that you can use to look at the difference in prices of currency and use a scale to measure it. This too requires you to conduct an in-depth statistical calculation which you can easily do using a simple software. The software will give you a quick result, and you won't have to do all the calculations.

Fibonacci retracements

If you are aware of the Fibonacci number sequence, then you will find this technique easy to adopt. It makes use of the Fibonacci number sequence to find the trend that the currency will follow. It is a predictive approach and is meant to help to understand whether or not the currency pairs will prove to be a lucrative investment.

These form the different technical analysis that you can perform to understand the trend of the currencies.

Sentimental analysis

Sentimental analysis refers to understanding the sentiment of the investors in the market. You have to analyze their mood and see what they are thinking about a certain currency. Whether they are interested in buying it or they wish to steer clear of it. You have to understand the course that they will take in order to make your own decision. In general, you have to follow the crowd if you wish to make a safe investment. But if you want to do something different then you should move against the crowd.

Forex hedging against inflation

It is obvious that every investor will worry about the inflation at some point in time or the other. For this, the trader can indulge in hedging. Hedging refers to protecting the investment from potential future losses. The trader will buy an asset that is priced much higher. That way, even if the value of the currency decreases then the trader can safeguard the investment. Forex is often compared with gold investments as the two provide similar protection against inflation.

Chapter 5: Will Bitcoin takes over the US Dollar?

For years, the US Dollar has reigned as the World's most widely used and widely held currency. The monetary equivalent of a global heart that keeps the blood of trade flowing. However, more recently this status has begun to wane. Some say that this could be the beginning of a trend that sees other currencies and assets taking its place. Bad news? Well, that all depends on who you are and what you own. So, if you hold Bitcoin or are thinking of investing in it, then you cannot afford to miss what I'm about to share with you. The Dollar is an asset and its value is of course determined by its price. So how has that price been doing recently? Well, not too good. The best way to get a sense of the value of a currency is to compare it to that of its global trading partners. This is why we have the US Dollar index. The US Dollar index is it's just a measure of the exchange rate of USD to a basket of currencies of the US's global trading partners. This index has been on a sustained decline since the beginning of 2020. In effect it is down by over 10 percent since the beginning of March 2020. What was driving this? Well, it comes down to one of the most fundamental economic disciplines of all; supply and demand. Like Newton's law of gravity, these economic principles apply to everything including the World's reserve currency. As we know from economics, the balance between the supply and demand of an asset impacts on the price of the asset. In the case of a currency, it's the price of said currency in relation to others, hence the Dollar index. What is known from this then is that there has been an overflow of Dollars on the open marketplace with a demand that has not been capable to keep up with it. When viewed in that framework, it makes sense as to why the Dollar index is on the degeneration. There has been a rapid decline in US economic activity from the pandemic. This has meant that the natural utility demand for Dollars has been on the decline too. Nonetheless, in order to respond to the falling economic activity, the FED has turned on those printing presses. Bond buying programs and quantitative easing have meant that we have had unprecedented levels of monetary stimulus that has flooded the system with Dollars. More Dollars floating around with less demand, therefore means that the price will of course react. This is what has been driving that decline in the Dollar index there. What is important to note here though, is that this US Dollar index is a separate concept to inflation, although they are quite related. Inflation is just a comparison of the purchasing power of US Dollars to general goods and services, whereas the USD index is a comparison to other currencies. A Dollar that's weak compared to other currencies will make imports more expensive, which could of course also drive inflation. What's most important to note here, is that those people who have kept hold of US Dollars in their bank accounts have held a rapidly depreciating asset. The most important question that we need to ask ourselves is whether this is likely to continue. Well, there are a number of global macroeconomic factors that we have to look at. Factors that impact not only on the supply and demand of USD, but also this relative to other currencies. So let's start on one of the biggest and longest running drags on the currency and that is the widening trade deficit. Quite simply, the trade deficit is the difference between a country's exports and imports. Some countries may run a deficit while others have a surplus when it comes to the United States, they run a pretty large deficit of close to 540 billion Dollars. This has worsened even more since the beginning of the Covid virus, as the US opened its economy and consumers started importing goods and services. The deterioration in the current account in the second quarter of last year was the worst on record. Now the US runs a deficit with a number of countries but perhaps the biggest deficits that it runs are with China, Japan and Germany. So why is a trade deficit bad for the US Dollar? Well, if people in the US are trade in more goods and services from overseas, then they are going to be paying for this in USD. This means that those countries that are exporting to these customers will have to convert that USD into their native currency to meet their costs. This therefore means that you have a lot of selling pressure on Dollars, which of course drives down the price. That's where we are right now, but is this likely to continue? Well, I happen to think so. This is just part of the trend in the decline of US manufacturing. China has now become the main manufacturing hub in the World, which means that the US will still have to import from them. Moreover, if the numerous tariffs and barriers that Trump put up against China could not reverse the trend, then it's hard to see how Biden could top that. The only thing that could possibly slow this could be for the US to become more competitive when it comes to manufacturing. But structurally changing the US labor market is not something that can happen in a year or two, and this is just the goods component of the balance of payments deficit. You should also consider the capital component. Given that there's been an explosion in government spending and a lack of domestic saving, the US has to import surplus savings from abroad if it wants to invest and grow. The United States budget deficit is now so steep that it will be hard for them to save domestically anytime in a little while. They must import those savings and reserves. It doesn't look like things are going to be improving on the balance of payment side for quite some time. But there is another far more consequential factor that has been driving Dollar depreciation recently and that is its general oversupply. The amount of money that's been pumped into the system is truly astounding. Last year a fifth of all US money supply was printed in a single year. In its entire 107 year history, 20% of all the money in circulation was printed in 2020. I don't need to tell you what effect this has on the value of the US Dollar. Oversupply with limited demand of course decreases its value. This is not only for purchasing power and inflation, but also its value relative to other currencies; depreciation. We know that the FED has had a hand in decreasing the value of the Dollar, but is this likely to continue? Well, it seems like it may, at least for the near term. In a latest virtual summit, Powell said that monetary stimulus will remain in place well into the recovery. Given that the recovery seems to have stalled more recently, one can therefore assume that the printing presses won't be slowed anytime soon. Currently, the FED is buying 120 billion Dollars of treasuries and mortgage-backed securities every month. 120 billion Dllars of extra funds that are likely to continue for the next few months. What all this means therefore is an increasing oversupply of the US Dollar and hence a fall in its value relative to other moneys. That will be the inevitable inflation that we could face once we emerge from the pandemic. This surge of jumbo jet money is going to be a strong headwind for the US Dollar in the coming months. Nonetheless there is one more reason that could have a further drag on its value and that is its global use. More specifically, its use in trade and as a reserve currency. Ever since the inception of the Bretton Woods system back in 1944, the US Dollar has been viewed as the global reserve currency. In fact, up until 1971, all other currencies were pegged to the Dollar at a fixed rate. Yet, things have changed considerably since then. As other states have sought to limit their reliance on the USD, so too has its global use waned. This has been triggered by the pandemic and more hostile trade practices. For example, in October 2020, the Euro exceeded the Dollar as the most used currency for global payments. Something that has not happened for years, and it seems as if this trend is likely to continue. That's because the EU is now making a concerted effort to steer most European settlements towards the Euro. More recently, the European Commission has outlined plans to increase the role of the Euro in international payments and investments. For example, they're going to be offering incentives for European market participants to work with currency clearing houses that are based in Europe, and the Europeans are not alone in this. Both China and Russia have indicated that they would like to move away from their dependence on US Dollar settlement, and this was even before the pandemic and tumultuous geopolitics of the past year. What all this shows

US is that demand to use greenbacks as a means to grease the wheels of global finance and trade, is likely to diminish over the coming years. As this transactional demand starts to wane so will its price relative to other currencies. This is just the use of Dollars as a medium of exchange. We should also not forget that Dollars are held by foreign central banks as a buffer to protect themselves. You can think of this as the investment demand for US Dollars. Here is a graph that shows US the US Dollar percentage of global reserve currencies.

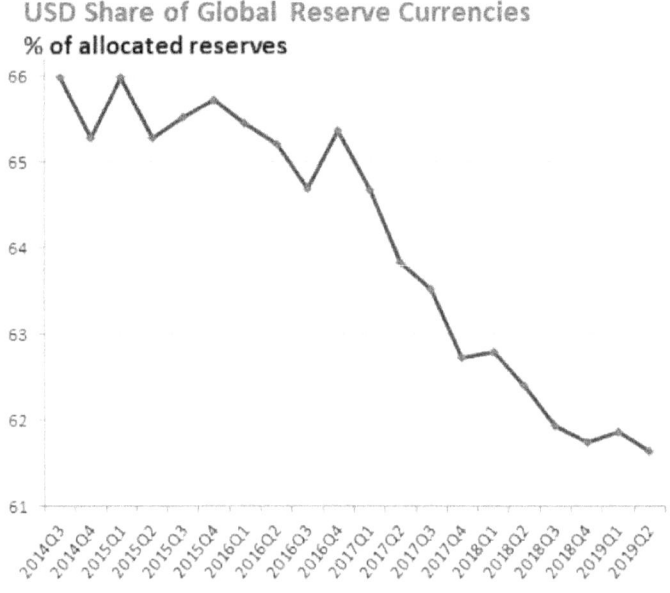

As you can see, there's been a sustained fall in this share

over the past seven years. Much of this comes down to those same geopolitical concerns that I just mentioned, but apart from that, it just makes practical sense. Why would a foreign central bank want to hold a currency, where the value of said currency can be easily impacted by the actions of the FED? Moreover, these central banks are banking on the continued solvency and strength of the US fiscals, both of which can sometimes be considered dubious. Furthermore, times have changed quite considerably for some of the largest central banks. Gone are the days when there were no reasonable alternatives to the US Dollar. Other global currencies such as the Yen, Euro and Sterling have gained market share and take a look at the growth of Chinese RMB use. That's a pretty substantial increase which came on the heels of RMB becoming an official reserve currency in 2016. It's not only been currency that these banks have been diversifying into; they've also been net buyers of gold ever since 2010. What all this means is that there's less central bank demand out there for US Dollars. Less demand to use it as a store of value. If we couple this with all of the other factors that I mentioned above, it's no surprise that the value of US Dollars has been on the decline. That's my prediction for the trajectory of the US Dollar. But fear not because I'm going to tell you why this decline in the US Dollar is the single most bullish factor that could supercharge Bitcoin. It's no longer a pipe dream. Bitcoin is emerging as one of the best bets against the declining value of the US Dollar. This is thanks to the many characteristics that make it such an amazing store of value. Limited supply, immutability and transparency. It's actually emerged as a theme among these investors. Bitcoin is an inflation and Dollar hedge that can be used to protect your wealth from these sustained trends. Firms on Wall Street are making the distinct connection between Dollar weakness, inflation and Bitcoin. These include the likes of JP Morgan, Paul Tudor Jones, Blackrock and the list goes on. You only need to take a look at the immense amount of institutional adoption that we've seen over the past year. I know what you're thinking; these are high alpha driven risk-taking Wall Streeters - of course they're comfortable with Bitcoin. Well, last year it was also announced that MassMutual an insurance fund was picking up Bitcoin. Insurance funds are much more risk-averse than your traditional money manager, and much more recently, it was disclosed that the endowments of Harvard, Yale, Brown and the University of Michigan have started buying Bitcoin. Now take a second to think about that; funds that are tasked with preserving capital for generations are investing in Bitcoin. They are a completely different investor class that's focused on steady growth and capital preservation. They're mostly global macro focused and are investing in Bitcoin based on global trends, one of which is of course hedging US Dollar devaluation. If you have Ivy League UNI Endowment funds investing in Bitcoin, how long do you think before pension funds start dipping their toes. Their investment profile is not that far removed, and Wall Street has already started building the infrastructure required in order to service these large investors needs. Take a look at all the banks and asset managers that are starting to offer Bitcoin custody solutions. Blackrock, Fidelity and even Goldman Sachs. Or, how about regulated investment funds? We all know about the explosive growth in AUM at Greyscale, but there are a number of other funds that have opened their doors. Let's also not forget that there's a raft of Bitcoin ETF applications that have been filed. We also have a more crypto friendly SEC and if one of these is approved, it will give a whole swathe of new investors an opportunity to buy into Bitcoin. This is all known and of course extremely positive for Bitcoin. But there is one investor class that could have an interest in buying some of that digital gold and it's one that I've just alluded to. There is a fairly decent chance that we could see a foreign central bank start allocating some of its reserves towards Bitcoin. It's only logical. It's a strong Dollar and inflation hedge and would allow them to diversify, away from the concept of foreign currency fiat reserves entirely. These central banks are more than willing to invest in gold as a store of value. However the latter beats the former. When it comes to a central bank, the main benefits of Bitcoin come with its ease of storage and conversion. There's no need to rely on a bank to hold cash or a vault to hold gold. A simple hardware device could theoretically hold the keys to the reserves of an entire central bank. It's not just me that thinks that central banks could dip their toes in these waters. The guys over at Masari mentioned it as a possibility in their 2021 crypto investment thesis. They see it as potentially appealing to central banks of those smaller EM currencies that are quite volatile. Still think it's a pipe dream? Well here is the ex-prime minister of Canada; actually referring to Bitcoin as an alternative reserve currency to the US Dollar. Reference:

https://uk.finance.yahoo.com/news/former-canadian-prime-minister-lists-140947075.html

The amount of Dollars currently held in reserves by these foreign central banks is immense. A tiny bit of diversification with a few of these banks could skyrocket the price of Bitcoin. That's just because there is very little of it to go around. It's quite clear that the value of the US Dollar is on the decline. While this trend may have been present before the pandemic, there's no doubt that it has triggered it. Furthermore, given many of the macroeconomic factors mentioned earlier, it looks like this trend is likely to continue at least for the foreseeable future. The current account deficit is growing. The FED is still printing. Foreign governments are diversifying and central banks are hedging. When combined these forces, don't seem to paint a pretty picture for USD. Of course, one man's pain is another man's gain. Dollar hedges are likely to become extremely popular. This is especially the case when devaluation is combined with broader inflation. Bitcoin is perhaps one of the best Dollar hedges out there, and that is not an opinion; it's becoming common knowledge. You only need to take a look at all the institutions, corporates funds and endowments who have allocated parts of their portfolio to Bitcoin. The last piece of that puzzle may in fact be central banks. As we've witnessed with the corporates all you need is one of them to break the stereotype, to take the plunge and hopefully start a trend. If that trend does take hold, then grab and hold of your sets because this is going to be one crazy ride. That's my miserable overview of the Dollar but super bullish view of Bitcoin.

Chapter 6: Lending Protocol for Crypto Loans

When I'm out hunting for small cap altcoin gems, there are a number of things that I look for. Factors that when brought together substantially increase the chance that the pick will be bang on the money. These include factors such as solving a pressing problem, being one of the first to do it, while being built in a less saturated ecosystem that has a well-supported token and one of the most promising projects that I've recently found that meets these criteria is Litentry or Lit. In order to understand Litentry, you have to appreciate the problem that it's trying to solve. Simply, it all comes down to decentralized identity management. Essentially, how do you attach unique identities to certain users on a decentralized blockchain? How do you know that a particular wallet address with which you're dealing, is controlled by a unique individual? How can you tell who that individual is? Now, I know what you're thinking; crypto is about anonymity, no one needs to know who I am. Well, that's only partly true. There are certain limits to the potential that DeFi can achieve without being able to attach identities to addresses. For example how can we deal with things like lending and credit delegation. You can borrow funds in DeFi right now but all of these loans are heavily over-collateralized. To this day, I do not know of any DeFi protocol that offers lending functionality for loans below a minimum of 140% collateralization. This is mainly for a very simple point; you don't know who you're lending to. You have no recourse if they don't pay back the loan. You can't verify their DeFi credit record. So it's only logical that you're going to ask for more collateral than they're asking for the loan. On the credit delegation point, I am not going to stand a surety for anyone else on the blockchain unless I know who they are. But that's just one of the issues that comes without identity attribution. Another one comes to decentralized governance. Currently, most proof-of-stake blockchains have a governance model where token holdings determine the weight of someone's vote. You may think that the governance mechanism is decentralized because there are a number of different wallets, however you've no way of knowing whether those wallets are controlled by a small group of individuals. This is of course a risk as we know that centralization could lead to conflicts of interest, when it comes to voting systems. This is only one of the potential issues that I foresee when one cannot adequately determine how decentralized a protocol really is. For example, what about those cases where a project wants to issue a unique airdrop to all of those individuals who've used the network? We've seen numerous examples of this in the DeFi space including Uniswap and 1 inch. This is great and all but what they've done is that they've airdropped these tokens based on unique addresses and not unique identities. So what this basically means is that if you held more than one address that used any of these protocols, you all have gotten the airdrop to more than one address. But despite whether you think that it's fair or not, it's completely within the protocol defined rules. Some may use the rules to their advantage, but if there was a way for Uniswap to have been able to identify unique users, they could have sent the airdrop to only those they knew were unique. These are only some of the benefits that come from being able to identify identities on chain, and that is exactly where Litentry comes in. Litentry is a project that's developing a platform to aggregate and manage Decentralized Identifiers or DIDs across numerous different blockchains. Basically a platform for projects and protocols to manage and use DIDs as an input into new and exciting features. More importantly, Litentry is trying to build a protocol that will allow these DIDs to be used privately and securely. When it comes to the underlying network, Litentry is built on Substrate. Substrate is a framework for building decentralized blockchains. Highly efficient and easy to build on. However one of the most exciting things about building on Substrate is that it is natively compatible with Polkadot. That means that it could eventually be launched as a Parachain on the Polkadot network. The benefits of this are immense. Ethereum is going through some severe scaling issues currently and until Ethereum 2.0 is launched, things are unlikely to improve much. Polkadot will be much more scalable than Ethereum, given the unique nature of its consensus mechanism. Moreover, through this unique Parachain architecture it means that DAPps built on Polkadot Parachains are interoperable. They can be used across a number of other blockchains and ecosystems. There is of course a lot more to Polkadot than this. What's important to know is what this means for Litentry. It means that it can be used for cross-chain identity management. It does not have to be restricted to merely the

Polkadot ecosystem. This means that DAPps that are built on Ethereum. Cosmos or Filecoin can make use of the did system developed by Litentry. DAPps like Compound, Uniswap and AAve could use Litentry crosschain identity services to expand their product lines. For example, there are credit delegation in AAve too. This basically would mean that someone could backstop the credit for someone else on the AAve platform. Though given that there is no way of confirming the identity and credit record of these users natively, they had to outsource this to the open law smart contracts. That being said if they were able to use a service like Litentry, this could be done seamlessly and on chain. They would be able to immediately verify the decentralized credit record of the counterparty in a private and secure way. Litentry sounds exciting, but how does it work? Let's take a high level look at the Litentry architecture. Firstly let's take a look at the user side technology and the primary piece of technology here is the Litentry mobile app. The app will be integrated with the latency network and will allow users to participate in the governance process and access identity-based services. The app could also be linked to other networks and even some traditional identity verification systems like LinkedIn. They will also be able to manage lit incentives here and also use it as a crypto wallet. The app will include the Litentry authenticator. This is the mobile identity and data hub for the web 3.0 ecosystem. You can actually get a sense of how this looks over on the initial proposal of the app over in their docs. They also have a github repo dedicated to the app that you can view as well. What's pretty neat is that you can actually also try out some features on late entry right now over with their DAPp playground. This is basically a hub of decentralized web applications built on Litentry. It demonstrates how the two-factor authentication will work. You can use it with no passwords or registration just to get a sense of how the tech will function. That's the user side features, however the real hardcore tech that's been developed is over on the developer side. Firstly, you have the core Litentry network. This is built on Substrate and hence uses one of the most well-known frameworks out there. A framework that includes some of the most robust and efficient byzantine consensus mechanisms. On a more technical level, the Litentry runtime protocol will be able to link an account across all other chains, using that unique identifier. The users on Litentry can sign transactions attached to their unique identity with a private key. The benefits of this are that the user data can be shared but privately. Nothing about the user themselves apart from the unique identifier is actually shared. This identifier can also be linked to on-chain crypto assets to verify information relevant for credit delegation. The exact mechanics of how Litentry network works is beyond the scope of this book. The most important thing to take away from this substrate architecture is the ability to easily upgrade to become a Parachain on the Polkadot ecosystem. Something else that Litentry is building in their tech stack is an SDK or Software Development Kit. This will be essential in order to encourage developers to build client-side applications on top of Litentry network. These currently support Javascript which is one of the most popular programming language out there, so that would ease developer adoption on the network. I should also note that in Litentry whitepaper they say that they're planning to add more language support to these SDKs, and one final piece of the latency architecture is their Light Client Services. These basically enable the Litentry mobile applications to be independent of third-party servers. More technically, it means that these apps can connect directly to the Litentry blockchain without having to rely on any single node. This of course has benefits when it comes to trust and decentralization. It prevents any situation where malicious nodes can feed false information to the clients. That's a bit of an overview of the Litentry architecture. Something that is no doubt central to the Litentry network and ecosystem is that Lit token. Lit is the native utility token on the Litentry network and performs a number of different functions. Firstly, it's used to pay for fees. There are a number of different fees that users will have to pay on the network. These include fees such as transaction fees to prevent spamming of the network, matching fees which are paid by applications to identity stakers; this incentivizes more people to stake identities on the network, validation fees paid to what are termed identity guardians who take responsibility for validating staking identities and ordering the data into an acceptable format. So, that's the utility generated from fees on the network, but Lit tokens are also used for staking purposes. Identity registrars are third parties that can set up indexed identity databases. These databases are then queried for the decentralized identifiers. In order to make sure that these registrars have skin in the game, they have monetary incentives and disincentives. This means that if there's any dishonest behaviour, they will have their stakes slashed or lost. Of course, they'll also earn rewards from providing these identity services. These block rewards for the stakers are paid in Lit. I should also note that because Lit will have economic value within a DeFi ecosystem. It can also be used as collateral. For example, if someone with an identity verifier on the lit entry network wants to lend some crypto, then they can deposit Lit as the collateral, so that's another form of utility right there. And of course, as is the case with most DeFi protocols, Lit will also be used in the decentralized governance of the protocol. It will determine the voting power of the individuals on the network. This could be decisions like functionality to add to the network or whether to remove any dishonest guardians. One more use case that they'll be for, Lit tokens is to be a grant that the team allocates two developers that build on Litentry, so as an incentive mechanism. Given that these developers have been rewarded an economic piece of the network, they will earn those rewards. Litentry has developed quite a lot of use cases for their token. I've not seen many projects at this stage of development that have structured such a comprehensive ecosystem for their tokens, but in order to understand its long-term potential, we have to take a look at the tokenomics. Firstly, let's start off with the initial distribution of the tokens. There is a total supply of 100 million Lit. These tokens were split according to the following; 15% to the Litentry team, 8% went to the seed investors, 12% to private sale and further sales, 17% will be reserved for the foundation to be used as grants, 3% to Binance launch pool and a full 45% to remain as network incentives in the Parachain auction system. When it comes to initial distribution, I think this is reasonably fair. If we include the founder allocation into the broader network incentives bucket, including launch pool, it's a full 65% that will eventually be released to the community. What's important though from an investment perspective is to determine potential supply headwinds from token unlock schedules. Users are no doubt concerned about the potential for initial sales to be dumped on the market. Well, the initial release is reasonable with steady unlock periods every quarter. In other words, there are no large release cliffs which could flood the markets with supply. The 3% released during the Binance launch pool has already been distributed and are in circulating supply. The Parachain auctions and block reward inflation will only start in November of 2025. Once the block rewards start, the rate of inflation will be determined by the amount that's staked on the network. The target network participation rate is 70% which would imply a 5% inflation rate. This is actually quite mild for a proof-of-stake blockchain. So from a supply perspective, Lit is unlikely to face either supply saturation or extensive inflation. All positive for long-term price appreciation. Of course, we also cannot forget that price is a function of supply and demand, and demand is likely to be quite strong for Lid. What makes me think this? Well, firstly from a protocol design perspective, the more the network is used, the more utility demand there will be for the token. The more demand there is to stake identities to pay for computations and to be used as collateral for lending services. There are no projects that currently provide similar services to Litentry, so when they do eventually launch there will be extensive demand for these decentralized identity services in the DeFi space. It's only logical. Then we also have to consider investment demand. Lit has already crossed a major hurdle by being listed on tier one exchange. Since Lit came out, the launch pool and the token began trading. The volume took off like crazy along with the price. There was a lot of demand to hodl' Lit and I think that this is likely to gain momentum. This is due to a number of factors. Firstly you have to consider that it's a project that will be launched as a Parachain on Polkadot. You only need to take a look at some of the excitement around Polkadot-based projects to get a sense of how much untapped demand there is here. There is a growing sense that DeFi tokens based on Polkadot could see similar price appreciation to those we saw in the Ethereum ecosystem back in 2020. As long as the market believes that, price momentum is likely to pick up. Finally, is also important to point out the fact that Litentry has its roots in Asia. For example the team is from China and most of the VC backers are from countries such as China and Vietnam. Investors in these regions tend to be more blockchain and crypto crazy than those in the west. This means that once Litentry is launched, there could be an immense frenzy from buyers in this region to pick up the tokens. What really drew me to Litentry was the problem that they're solving in the DeFi space. I had not seen or heard about a project that was offering similar identity-based verifications in any ecosystem. Being able to verify the unique identity of wallet addresses, is the missing key to DeFi offering many of the other services that centralized finance relies on. Under collateralized lending and credit delegation are features that are just not on the DeFi menu yet. Not until we can verify identities and even then, DeFi currently lacks the mechanisms to fully identify how decentralized their networks are. All of these problems can be solved with Litentry's technology. Moreover, given that it could be upgraded to a Polkadot Parachain, this means that it will be built on one of the most exciting ecosystems in the crypto space right now. Scalable, interoperable and highly functional. Something else I really liked about the Litentry team is how much work has been done on the idea already. Unlike many other early stage projects that try to raise millions on nothing more than a white paper, these guys have already built numerous concepts and pushed hundreds of lines of code. All completely free to explore in their github repos. I should also note that Litentry has a really exciting roadmap, both for their runtime development and their mobile application, so there's a lot to look forward to on the tech front over the coming months. Apart from that, I like the tokenomics of Lit. It seems that they've attempted to cover all bases and create real utility value for the token. Add to that the fact that supply growth is relatively mild and there is a reasonable token unlock schedule. Of course it also helps that there's a great deal of demand to hodl' Lit. There is a strong community that has already rallied behind it and as we know community engagement helps to drive buzz around the project. Are there risks? Well, of course, there always are. There is a risk that the project does not launch on a Parachain. There is a risk that a competing protocol does it better. There is a risk of a security breach in the future that could expose personal info on chain. But these risks are all known and have been incorporated into my risk reward analysis. But remember, you will have to decide whether it fits your personal risk profile.

Chapter 7: Cryptocurrencies

Cryptocurrencies have gained immense popularity in the past decade. They have been endorsed by central banks, global financial institutions, and even social media giants. Their popularity has been built on their distinct features and characteristics.

A cryptocurrency is a virtual currency that is essentially a software created by performing complex mathematical calculations as dictated by code. The process operates over a network that involves several computers located throughout the world and is protected by a technology known as blockchain. Because the currency is protected by digital cryptography, it is unique in the sense that it cannot be counterfeited or spent twice. A major reason for the rise in popularity of cryptocurrencies is that unlike all other currencies, cryptocurrencies are not issued by any central bank. This makes cryptocurrencies immune to any manipulation by sovereign governments or central banks. Cryptocurrencies are protected using blockchain technology in such a way that their transfers are possible directly between two pirates without the need of a third party. Transfers of cryptocurrencies take several minutes but they have extremely low costs.

Because of the way cryptocurrencies are designed, they are by nature scarce and each new mined coin takes more resources. These contribute to a steady increase in prices which investors have attributed to the possibility of using cryptocurrencies as a hedge against inflation.

Note: A cryptocurrency investment is extremely speculative, and it's not recommended to invest more than 0.5-1% of your portfolio in crypto.

Bitcoin as an Asset Class and an Investment

Bitcoins are a unique payment system and a form of a reward for a process known as mining, and is primarily used in the exchange of products, services, or currencies. Bitcoins are the pioneer of a decentralized peer-to-peer payment system with no third parties involved. Bitcoins were the first execution of a concept under the name of "cryptocurrency" that was speculated and surfaced over a cypherpunks mailing list in 1998. The proposed idea meant a new form of money using cryptography (rather than middlemen or a central authority) to administer its transactions and creations. The design was finally implemented in 2009 after the bitcoin software was applied as open-source code (OSS). Its popularity has grown in the past decade as developers continue to work on its development.

Bitcoins are owned by no central authority and are rather controlled by bitcoin users worldwide. Bitcoin development is limited to improving the technology without enabling a change in the bitcoin protocol. Users can use any version or software but to remain compatible with each other similar rules must be applied for a uniform crypto network.

The backend network of Bitcoins is much more complicated than how users view it as a mere computer program. It shares 'blockchain' technology, which is a public ledger. The ledger enables the user's computer to verify how viable each bitcoin is for every transaction that takes place. Digital signatures protect each Bitcoin transaction allowing users to use their Bitcoin addresses to exchange Bitcoins. Additionally, Bitcoin mining refers to the process that produces more bitcoins by solving a computational puzzle, rewarding the miner with bitcoins in return.

The electronic cash system is recognized as a standard representation of a cryptocurrency and happens to be the most popular digital currency. Bitcoins are used by individuals worldwide. In 2017 alone there were up to approximately 5.8 million cryptocurrency wallet users, of which a large fraction were bitcoin users, as per a research conducted by the University of Cambridge.

The value of Bitcoin consistently appreciates over the long term although it has experienced an exceptional level of volatility over the years. Bitcoins that could be purchased for $0.0008-$0.8$ per Bitcoin are now valued at $39,334.20 each (8th January 2021). Bitcoin gained its value due its rising demand and limited supply. The negative correlation between the supply and demand of bitcoins is what drives the price up. Over time Bitcoins have matured in the crypto industry, gaining the attention of investors as it is increasingly being looked upon as a credible derivative that can be used as a hedge against inflation.

Bitcoins possess the largest market capitalization of any cryptocurrency today. Most economists regard bitcoins as a top-performing asset class with the unique traits it holds. However, a consensus on the nature of bitcoins remains undecided.

With the growing popularity of bitcoins as well as the rise of their value due to limited supply, investors are more convinced than ever to own bitcoins. Investment decisions can strongly rely on bitcoins' nature, making it essential to establish a consensus on whether bitcoins represent a new asset class.

Bitcoins are now being regulated in various jurisdictions worldwide that comply with local and international laws and allow investors to purchase bitcoins through established exchanges or crypto platforms legally.

The return on bitcoins and the risk-reward associated with it requires conclusions drawn from statistical approaches. Bitcoins have shown an insignificant correlation with other asset class traits. It is not associated with regular stocks or commodities as it goes in the normal world.

Despite bitcoins being relatively new in the market, the returns consistently outsize the preceding year's figures since crypto had begun and are now seen increasingly as suitable hedge against inflation. Bitcoins are an ideal investment primarily due to their fixed supply that stores value and contains enough potential to appreciate in the long run. Investment banks and institutional investors are consistently piling into the use of cryptocurrencies.

Litecoin and Ethereum

Cryptocurrencies are not limited to the use of bitcoins. There are several other investment options that investors opt for depending on their trading style and bankroll. Some prominent alternatives to cryptocurrencies apart from bitcoins are Ethereum and Litecoin.

Ethereum

Ethereum is a software platform designed in 2015 to serve the purpose of supporting decentralized contracts and digital cash. With a market cap of $69,604,579,809 (1/10 the size of bitcoins), Ethereum is the closest alternative to bitcoins one can find.

It is speculated that Ethereum holds the potential to revolutionize data protection, the finance industry, and social media. It also claims to secure, codify, and trade anything. It has gained support from significant financial organizations such as Microsoft Azure and Amazon Web Services.

Litecoin

Another well-versed option in the crypto market is Litecoin, referred to as the silver to bitcoin's gold. Litecoin is an open-source and decentralized software that is a form of digital cash.

Litecoin transaction fees are relatively lower, considering it requires minimal resources. Litecoin also tops bitcoin with a processing speed that is four times faster, posing as an ideal option in terms of efficiency and costs.

The future of Litecoin depicts a potentially good investment for most investors and is regarded as a close call to bitcoins.

Historical Performance Against Inflation

In 2009 when the initial trading of bitcoins had begun, the

digital cryptocurrency had undergone a lot of volatility. The fluctuations in price were seen in 2010 when the value of a single bitcoin rose from $0.0008 to $0.8. Since then, bitcoins have experienced significant crashes and rallies. Mt.Gox surfaced into a marketplace for bitcoins, having 150,000 bitcoins exchanged every day. However, due to its volatile nature and speculations for fraud the exchange was taken down in 2013. By 2020 Bitcoins were able to regain its losses which were previously incurred and possess a market cap of over $732 billion as of January 8th, 2020. It is now traded on numerous licensed and credible exchanges such as Kraken, Coinbase and Gemini.

Bitcoins are carefully designed with a deflationary approach, in addition to being a unit that stores value. It represents a similar gold standard creating opportunities for crypto users and investors to rise above the adverse effects of inflation.

Bitcoins are popular for their incredible potential to provide industries with protection against inflation and pose as an inflationary hedge, encouraging investors to own more bitcoins. Tycoon investors refer to bitcoins as the new gold for the 21 century and consider them as being naturally immune to the impacts of inflation.

The performance of bitcoins against the global pandemic tells us a lot about the potential of bitcoins against inflation. COVID-19 measures had led to the implementation of an inflationary monetary policy, which encouraged an aggressive supply. The lockdowns measures had given rise to key areas and food staples, largely affecting businesses worldwide (Similar to the 1970s when the USA encountered massive unemployment, which led to gold being the currency savior against inflation)

Bitcoin happens to be an ideal hedge against inflation in this scenario. Bitcoins possess a natural inflationary trait with a fixed 21 million bitcoin supply. This limit is what drives the value of bitcoins up and makes them immune to monetary inflation.

The supply shortage against the rising demand for bitcoins depicts an increase in the future per unit price which is gaining the attention of investors worldwide.

Prospects as a Hedge Against Inflation

The limited supply of bitcoins creates an inflation hedge, unique to other asset classes as it is immune to the changes of a political environment within a country. Investors that purchase bitcoins are not intending to contribute to a deflationary measure but are using it as a hedge against the consequences of inflation. However, despite the benefits cryptocurrencies are speculative and highly volatile. In the worst-case scenario, investors may even lose all their money rather than gaining anything.

Apart from inflation, bitcoins also pose as a hindrance against a disruptive law and order due to political instability. The prospects of bitcoins seek potential in preventing additional factors that can trigger more inflation.

Police states practicing seizure of private wealth and bank accounts closing due to unreliable governments can be minimized with bitcoins. Corrupted systems, export-protecting devaluations are namely few inflation triggers that bitcoins act as a hedge against.

Chapter 8: Worst case scenario - Hyperinflation

We have already discussed inflation at length throughout this book. It is a reduction in the purchasing power of a currency. Hyperinflation is accelerated version of inflation. When the rate of inflation is exceedingly high, usually over 50%, an economy is considered to experience hyperinflation. It quickly erodes the purchasing power of a local currency, significantly raises prices for goods, and causes the value of savings to drop dramatically. It usually occurs in extenuating circumstances such as war or an abject failure of economic policy. Because the rate of inflation increases rapidly during times of hyperinflation, the rates are usually measured on a daily basis. These daily rates sometimes fall between 5% and 10%. When the monthly CPI goes over 50%, an economy experiences hyperinflation.

What causes hyperinflation?

Hyperinflation is usually caused by an excessive money supply or an extreme lack of confidence in a country's currency by its citizens and trading partners. The most common reason for hyperinflation is when a central bank starts printing excessive amounts of money for one reason or the other. This is usually a result of an economic depression. An economic depression is different to a recession in the sense that it lasts much longer, usually a couple of years. Because of this, the central bank decides to pump more money into the economy to stimulate economic activity to get out of depression. However, sometimes the rise in money supply is not met with a proportionate rise in economic output. Due to ensuing depression, businesses increase the prices of goods and services in order to remain profitable. These increases are met by purchases because people have the money to buy them. Because the central bank continues to print more money, consumers continue to purchase products with ever increasing prices. As a consequence, hyperinflation takes hold.

Another reason that causes hyperinflation is when a local population does have the same confidence in the value of a currency as before. When this happens, a constant low confidence environment spreads across the population. People start buying goods in more quantities than they do in anticipation of rising prices. This causes more people to start buying even more things for fear of missing out on essential goods and services. This causes prices to get out of control sometimes and hyperinflation occurs.

Options for Hyperinflation

If you ever find yourself in a country that is either experiencing hyperinflation, or it might soon, there are various steps you can take to protect yourself. As hyperinflation significantly erodes the value of the currency, commodities become expensive. The most in-demand items such as food, water, fuel, and utilities usually experience the highest increase in prices. Owning assets that produce these commodities, or owning these commodities outright is an excellent way to insulate yourself from the harmful effects of hyperinflation.

A lot of the strategies listed below are from the people who experienced hyperinflation in the Weimar Republic post World War I. This was the last case of hyperinflation in a developed country.

Owning Farmland or a Home Garden

There are several assets investors choose to turn to

whenever investing in balancing out the effects of inflation. Gold is a popular and effective asset to consider. However, investing in a commodity such as owning farmland or home garden can pay off better than other asset classes.

In other words, the rising prices in food and other organics play a significant role in inflation. To benefit from this, investors invest in farmlands that pay off better during inflation. Higher prices would increase the value for crops, allowing the farmer to make up for higher rent expenses for the land.

Investors are more inclined than ever in owning home gardens or farmlands as the demand for food continues to rise while farmland supply decreases significantly. Investing in farmland is profitable as it offers constant returns as per historical evidence and effectively poses as a hedge against inflation measures.

Farmland is referred to as gold that can yield. Such an investment enables investors to be more exposed to opportunities for financial gain. The valuable commodities that are produced from the farmland give an edge over investing in other options available.

Converting Everything to Foreign Currency or Precious Metals

During hyperinflation, the average value of a country's currency decreases notably. Converting existing cash or owning foreign currency(ies) or precious metals is the smart option to opt for during hyperinflation. Owning top-performing assets can act as a hedge against hyperinflation and its severe consequences. In some cases, it might even be very profitable. Investors have been using the tactic of investing in precious metals to prevent themselves from adverse risks and financial repercussions.

The prices of precious metals rise higher during inflation and are relatively safe compared to other asset classes. Investors who sense incoming hyperinflation are quick to respond by investing in metals like gold and silver.

As the currency value decreases, the value of precious metals increases, depicting a negative correlation. These metals balance out the effects of inflation giving investors an upper hand even during times of a financial crisis.

Similarly, local currency can quickly lose its value, and

investors often turn to store their money value by converting cash or liquid assets to foreign currencies. Converting everything into foreign currency can protect investors from the impacts of the devalued currency i.e., losing their current monetary value. The foreign exchange rates may vary based on the different inflation rates amongst the many currencies available.

Postponing Payment of Debt

With hyperinflation, you can expect to witness a decline in the average value of a country's currency that is undergoing a financial crisis. Money now is more valuable than what it will be in the future.

The value of debt decreases during hyperinflation; however, it can become quite challenging to pay off debts during hyperinflation. This is because inflation often has little to no effect on income. With a diminishing value of income, individuals will be spending more on sky-high goods and will have lesser disposable income to pay off debts. But delaying these payments will be a lot more beneficial since the debt will be worth less and less as the value of the local currency continues to decline.

A financial crisis would encourage businesses to delay payments by purchasing supplies on credit. These businesses prefer to delay their payment dates to incur a 'less valuable debt' during hyperinflation. Failure to obtain credit for a business during hyperinflation may be as severe as putting the firm out of business. You can also do the same and seek to delay payment of as much debt as is possible. This is because it will be a lot easier to pay off the debt in the future as the value of the currency in which the debt was taken would be significantly reduced. If you also invest in commodities or other assets to protect yourself against hyperinflation, you would be able to pay off the debt with much more ease in the future.

Getting into Long Term Financing

When an economy experiences hyperinflation, central banks usually raise interest rates to control inflation by reducing the money supply. This makes borrowing expensive in the short term. However, the important thing to note is that since all these loans will need to be paid back in the local currency, the loans will be worth much less in the future and consequently, much easier to pay off. This is because the currency would have significantly lost its value making it a lot easier to acquire from the sale of goods or property. For example, if you take out a mortgage from a bank in a period of an extremely high level of inflation, your monthly payments will be in the local currency. However, the value of your property will most likely appreciate monthly and will be worth many times more at the time of the mortgage's maturity. This is because you will be making the payments in the now heavily discounted local currency. A mortgage is one example. You can also take other forms of long-term financing. The basic idea is to buy commodities or assets that have the greatest potential of appreciating in value over time as the value of the currency in which the loan has been borrowed continues to decline.

The Risk of Government Intervention

During a traumatic experience like hyperinflation, there is tremendous pressure on the Government to mitigate the pain due to hyperinflation. This element is very unpredictable. For example, long term financing of apartments might make you think that it's a great think to be a landlord during hyperinflation. However, during the Weimar Republic hyperinflation, rents were capped by the Government, leading to many landlords going bust.

During hyperinflation in Venezuela, it's natural for wheat and soy prices to rise. However, the Government imposed price controls which led to food shortages.

In Argentina, the Government outlawed exchange of Argentinian pesos for foreign currency.

The anonymous and decentralized nature of Bitcoin has proven to be a boon for those who held Bitcoin in Venezuela. Venezuelans have widely adopted use of Bitcoin in their daily life through P2P (Peer-to-Peer) networks. Other countries with high inflation problems (like Zimbabwe) have struggled to do so.

The unknown elements of hyperinflation make diversification especially important. You never know what is an asset during hyperinflation, and what is not.

Conclusion

Sectors that Outperform during Inflationary Periods

We have talked at length about the types of sectors that have traditionally performed very well during inflationary periods. These sectors can be traced back to the fundamentals upon which inflation is based. These fundamentals dictate that sectors that deal with goods that are in demand all year round are very likely to perform well during times of inflation. The reason being their ability to transfer the increase in the cost of their raw materials directly onto consumers because people always need what they are selling. These sectors commonly include food and beverage producers, agriculture companies, and healthcare providers.

Other sectors that perform really well during inflationary periods are those sectors that either produce or provide services to utility companies and energy providers. Examples include power generation companies and oil and gas companies, These sectors experience healthy appreciation in their stock prices during times of high inflation because they are directly related to the core energy requirements of the population.

The Importance of Diversification in a Portfolio

While we have discussed numerous ways through which you can confidently protect your finances against inflation, we would suggest not putting all of your eggs in one basket. The main reason for this is that even though all of the avenues we have discussed are quite effective at countering the effects of inflation if they are used together, their effects can become more certain.

There are countless combinations you can try to create a diverse portfolio to protect your investments. This is my favorite allocation.

10% Precious metals

15% Commodities

20% High Quality Tech Investments

20% Foreign stocks (non-US developed and emerging)

10% Real estate (REIT's, REIM's)

10% Speculation (Crypto / Mining Stocks)

15% Cash in Multiple Currencies/Inflation Indexed Bonds

There are a few reasons why this specific combination is ideal.

- Firstly, because having stakes in commodities, tech investments, and foreign stocks ensure that more than 70% of your portfolio is highly liquid. This means that you can convert your holdings into and out of cash quickly and easily.

- Secondly, investing in precious metals, commodities, and real estate is almost guaranteed to perform well during inflationary periods even if the other assets in your portfolio do not or take a while to catch up with the others in terms of value appreciation.

- Thirdly, because investing 10% in speculative instruments provides a little risk exposure to your portfolio which can produce more than average results but even if it underperforms, it will still be only 10% or less which means that more than 90% of your portfolio will be relatively safer and will go on to ensure that the entire portfolio makes a decent return.

- And lastly, a 10% investment in real estate provides much-needed strength to the portfolio as real estate almost always performs well in the long term. Because this is not as liquid as the others, you will be less likely to trade it more frequently which will ensure that your portfolio has a long-term appreciating asset as well.

Thanks for reading Inflation911, I hope you understand the process better, and realize how much Inflation can impact your cash savings, assets and investment portfolio.

More importantly though, is to have a few basic strategies you can deploy when the US economy is experiencing covert Inflation that will protect your money and also increase it from the anomalies created by economic Inflation.

Lucas Heidel

www.ingramcontent.com/pod-product-compliance
Lightning Source LLC
Chambersburg PA
CBHW050009230526
45465CB00003BB/1327